S0-AQO-565

WILLIAMS · SONOMA

Juicer
COOKBOOK

Recipes by Carol Gelles

Photography by Karl Petzke

WILLIAMS-SONOMA
Founder and Vice-Chairman: Chuck Williams
Book Buyer: Victoria Kalish

WELDON OWEN INC.
President: John Owen
Vice President and Publisher: Wendely Harvey
Chief Operating Officer: Larry Partington
Vice President, International Sales: Stuart Laurence
Associate Publisher: Lisa Atwood
Managing Editor: Hannah Rahill
Consulting Editor: Norman Kolpas
Copy Editors: Sharon Silva, Carolyn Miller
Design: Kari Perin, Perin+Perin
Production Director: Stephanie Sherman
Production Manager: Jen Dalton
Editorial/Production Assistant: Cecily Upton
Food Stylist: Sandra Cook
Prop Stylist: Sara Slavin

In collaboration with Williams-Sonoma
3250 Van Ness, San Francisco, CA 94109

A WELDON OWEN PRODUCTION

Copyright © 1998 Weldon Owen Inc.
814 Montgomery St., San Francisco, CA 94133
All rights reserved, including the right of
reproduction in whole or in part in any form.
Library of Congress Cataloging-in-Publication Data
Gelles, Carol.
   Juicer : cookbook / recipes by Carol Gelles;
      photography by Karl Petzke.
      p. cm. -- (Williams-Sonoma Cookware Series)
   includes index.
   ISBN 1-887451-14-5
   1. Juicers. 2. Fruit juices. 3. Cookery (fruit).
      4. Vegetable juices. 5. Cookery (vegetables).
      I. Title. II. Series: Williams-Sonoma
      cookware.
TX840.J84G45   1998
641.8'75 -- dc21   97-47319 CIP
First printed in 1998
10 9 8 7 6 5 4 3 2 1

Production by Toppan Printing Co., (H.K.) Ltd.
Printed in China

A Note on Weights and Measures:
All recipes include customary U.S. and metric
measurements. Metric conversions are based on
a standard developed for these books and have
been rounded off. Actual weights may vary.

CONTENTS

Fresh fruit and vegetable juices with flavors, textures, and nutritional values that soar above those of bottled or canned juices. Wondrously aromatic marinades, dressings and sauces, stocks and soups. Healthy beverages for breakfast, lunch, or pre- or postworkout. Delectable granitas, mousses, and other desserts with just-harvested taste. These are just some of the gastronomic rewards made possible by owning a juicer.

The instructions and recipes in this book are designed to help you maximize your use of an electric juicer. They concentrate on the two most common types owned by home cooks today: the juice extractor and the citrus juicer.

An extractor is the most efficient tool for removing the juice from the widest range of fruits and vegetables. First, it reduces them to minute particles with its swiftly whirling shredding disk. Then it extracts liquid from the particles by centrifugal force, sending it through the fine mesh of a strainer basket that holds back the pulp, which itself can be utilized in some recipes to add fiber and texture.

Electric citrus juicers are simply mechanized versions of the oldest-known type of juicer, the reamer (right), which gouges and presses the juice from halved citrus fruits. Although they only work with citrus, these juicers are more reasonably priced than extractors. Some extractors come with citrus-juicing attachments, however, that function in the same way.

Whichever kind of juicer you use, the end product is guaranteed to satisfy. Once extracted, the flavors, aromas, and colors of juices are intensified. In the case of softer, smoothly textured produce, such as avocados and bananas, fine purées are the result. Plus, all the juices and purées emerge packed with readily accessible nutrients. You can even use leftover pulp for flavoring stocks or adding fiber to baked goods.

On the following pages you'll find detailed descriptions of the juice extractor and citrus juicer and how to use them, along with guidelines for selecting and preparing the most likely candidates for juicing. For the best result, start with the highest-quality seasonal produce at the peak of ripeness. Then, you'll be ready to prepare the delicious easy-to-make recipes that complete this book, each of which gains its special character and appeal from fresh juices.

a brief history

For centuries, ingenious cooks have found ways to extract the essence of fruits and vegetables. The most likely candidates for juicing, and therefore the objects of the earliest inventions, were citrus fruits, which gave up liquid all the more easily when halved and pressed against a ridged, cone-shaped reamer (below).

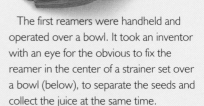

The first reamers were handheld and operated over a bowl. It took an inventor with an eye for the obvious to fix the reamer in the center of a strainer set over a bowl (below), to separate the seeds and collect the juice at the same time.

In the early 20th century, mechanized ingenuity came to bear, with lever-operated, rack-and-pinion citrus reamers—soda fountain fixtures—that juiced the fruit under close to a thousand pounds (500 kg) of pressure. (The same lever-operated concept, although without the force generated by a rack-and-pinion mechanism, is used in the whimsical bird juicer below.) Then, in the 1950s, motor-driven citrus juicers suitable for household use were introduced.

Still, until recent years, it remained hard to juice anything other than citrus fruits at home. The advent of relatively inexpensive models of the powerful juice extractors that have been fixtures in health-food stores for decades has changed the face of home juicing.

JUICE EXTRACTOR

When using any extractor-type juicer, follow the manufacturer's instructions for specifics on how your particular machine should be assembled and operated. Pay special attention to precautions regarding limiting the motor's running time, and to any safety locks that prevent children from operating it.

An extractor is driven by a heavy MOTOR that rapidly rotates a disk-shaped metal cutting blade covered with sharp-edged shredding holes. The blade, in turn, sits inside a fine-mesh STRAINER BASKET that spins along with the blade. Centrifugal force flings the finely shredded fruit or vegetable particles against the inner walls of the basket, forcing out their juices. These flow to a spout (beneath which a glass, measuring cup, or bowl should be positioned) at the bottom of a WORK BOWL that encloses both the blade and the basket and sits securely atop the motor base. A COVER, outfitted with a feed chute and a PLUNGER for introducing ingredients, snaps tightly on top of the bowl.

When juicing more than one type of fruit or vegetable, always feed harder or smoother-textured ingredients first. Follow them with more watery ingredients that will help flush them through, stopping regularly at both stages to clean out pulp and residue from the strainer.

Cover | Plunger

Strainer Basket

Work Bowl

Motor

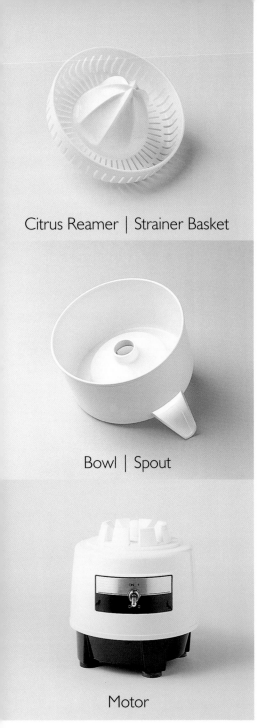

Citrus Reamer | Strainer Basket

Bowl | Spout

Motor

a note on safety

Whatever kind of juicer you have, be sure to review the instructions that accompanied it before you put it to use. Take care to assemble the juicer correctly and to keep your fingers and hands clear of any sharp or moving parts. For the most efficient and safe operation, clear out pulp frequently from the machine.

CITRUS JUICER

Whether you use a citrus juicer attachment on an extractor or a machine exclusively designed for citrus fruits, the basic function remains the same. In both cases, study the manufacturer's instructions before beginning, paying attention to the safety precautions. Always wash the bowl, reamer, and strainer basket before and after each use.

A citrus juicer, like an extractor, is driven by a heavy-duty MOTOR encased in a sturdy base. On top of the base sits a BOWL with a SPOUT, out of which the pressed juice flows and beneath which a glass, measuring cup, or bowl should be positioned before juicing begins. Inside the bowl, resting atop a post that extends from the motor, is the ridged, cone-shaped CITRUS REAMER. This, in turn, is surrounded by a STRAINER BASKET.

Once the machine has run for a few seconds to reach full speed, a citrus fruit half is firmly pushed, cut side down, onto the spinning reamer cone. The cone gouges out the pulp and presses out its juice. The strainer basket holds back the pulp, while the juice flows through into the bowl and out the spout into a waiting glass or other receptacle. If pulpier juice is preferred, simply remove some of the pulp from the strainer basket with a spoon and stir it into the juice.

These instructions explain the basics of selecting and preparing the most common fruits for juicing. Seek out fully ripened fruits at their peak of season. That said, juicing can be a good way to use specimens that are slightly past their prime; their juice will be sweeter and more easily extracted, and any mealiness in texture will not affect the flavor of the juice. Be sure to rinse fruits that don't require peeling under running water.

autumn tree fruits
(APPLES, PEARS)

Look for firm, hard apples; Red or Golden Delicious carry the sweetest juice. Ripe, ready pears give slightly to pressure. Core the fruit and cut into pieces that fit the extractor chute. The thin juices of the apples and pears oxidize quickly; use soon after juicing.

summer tree fruits
(APRICOTS, CHERRIES, NECTARINES, PEACHES, PLUMS)

Choose plump, firm but ripe fruits heavy for their size; avoid any with hard or mushy spots. Ripe nectarines and peaches will also have a sweet fragrance. Halve and pit the fruit. Juices will have a nectarlike consistency.

melons
(CANTALOUPE, HONEYDEW, WATERMELON)

Whole melons should feel heavy for their size; cantaloupes and honeydews will yield slightly to pressure at their blossom ends. Discard the rind and seeds and cut into chunks. Melon juices are thin and sweet.

tropical fruits
(BANANAS, KIWIFRUITS, MANGOES, PAPAYAS, PINEAPPLES)

Pick ripe, aromatic fruits that yield to gentle pressure. Peel off skins. Cut mango flesh from the pit; discard papaya seeds. Bananas, kiwifruits, mangoes, and papayas form purées. Pineapples yield a thin, sweet-tart juice.

grapes
(BLACK, GREEN, RED)

Select firm grapes that remain well attached to their stems and yield slightly to finger pressure; taste one to test for sweetness. Before juicing, rinse the grapes and then stem them; there is no need to seed them. Peeling grapes, although a tedious task, will eliminate any hint of bitter aftertaste.

berries
(BLACKBERRIES, BLUEBERRIES, CRANBERRIES, RASPBERRIES, STRAWBERRIES)

Buy plump, ripe berries without evident surface moisture; check carefully to eliminate any with even a trace of mold. Hull, if needed, before juicing. Juice will be fairly thick and, depending upon the berry, sweet to tart.

citrus fruits
(GRAPEFRUITS, LEMONS, LIMES, ORANGES)

Look for shiny-skinned, plump fruits heavy for their size that yield slightly to finger pressure; if possible, choose less expensive "juice oranges." Cut in half crosswise and juice with a citrus juicer. Or remove all peel, pith, and seeds and use an extractor.

These pages explain how to prepare various vegetables for juicing and describe the types of juice they yield. When juicing vegetables, bear in mind that most of them have highly distinctive flavors, making them suitable only for using in small amounts or in judicious combinations with other ingredients. When assembling a dish or beverage that uses two or more different juices, remember to start with the vegetables that yield thicker juices, following them with those that produce thinner ones that will flush out the machine. Select best-quality, peak-of-season produce, and be careful to avoid specimens that are over- or underripe or show signs of spoilage. Finally, if your budget allows, you might wish to seek out vegetables that have been grown without the use of pesticides or chemical fertilizers for a more healthful lifestyle.

stalks and shoots
(ASPARAGUS, CELERY, FENNEL)

Choose firm, crisp, fresh-looking specimens. Trim asparagus and celery; trim away fennel stems, leaves, and core, then cut the bulb into chunks. Juices will be thin. Asparagus tastes very strong, celery is neutral, and fennel has a licorice flavor.

cabbage family
(BROCCOLI, CABBAGE, CAULIFLOWER)

Look for firm, good-colored, unblemished specimens without any sign of limpness. Trim and cut broccoli and cauliflower into pieces that fit the chute; separate and roll up cabbage leaves. Juices will be fairly thin in consistency but strong in flavor.

roots and bulbs
(BEETS, CARROTS, GINGER, KOHLRABI, ONIONS, PARSNIPS)

Select firm, heavy, unblemished specimens. Cut off green tops and scraggly roots. Peel onions and parsnips; scrub other roots. The thin juices will resemble their source, from sweet carrot to sharp and spicy ginger.

vegetable fruits
(CUCUMBERS, PEPPERS, TOMATOES)

Choose firm, unblemished specimens. Before cutting into chunks, peel cucumbers; stem, seed, and derib peppers; and stem tomatoes. Cucumber juice is thin and mild, pepper juice is thin and flavorful, and tomato juice is thick and fresh tasting.

leaf vegetables
(GREENS, LETTUCES, PARSLEY)

Buy crisp, fresh-looking leaves. Separate the leaves, then fold or roll into compact shapes that fit the extractor's chute. Juices will be thin and their flavors will reflect the source, from mild for iceberg lettuce to fairly bitter for tougher, darker leaves such as beet greens or romaine (cos).

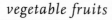

avocados

Ripe avocados yield slightly to gentle pressure. The dark, pebbly skinned Hass variety has the best flavor and texture. Halve the avocado, remove the pit, peel off the skin, and cut the flesh into pieces. The purée that results from juicing will be thick, smooth, and rich.

JUICES AND SMOOTHIES

Carrot Pineapple Orange Juice

SERVES 1

*This morning eye-opener provides an outstanding source
of vitamins A and C. If you drink it fresh from the extractor,
the orange and lemon rinds add a lovely, subtle flavor.
Otherwise, peel the orange and lemon before juicing, as the rinds
will make the juice bitter after sitting for an hour or two. Look
for ripe pineapple with a mild aroma and golden peel.*

1 small orange, including rind, seeded and
cut into pieces (see note)

$\frac{1}{8}$ small, ripe pineapple, peeled,
cored, and cut into pieces

2 carrots, scrubbed clean and cut into pieces

$\frac{1}{4}$ small lemon, including rind, seeded (see note)

In an extractor, juice the orange, pineapple, carrots, and lemon,
in that order. Stir and serve. ✳

17

Two-Berry Smoothie

SERVES 1

*Ripe, fresh seasonal fruit is the best choice for
this summery drink. If you have only frozen berries,
defrost them before juicing. You may not need to add the
sugar if the fruit is sweet. If you like, reserve
a few attractive berries and skewer them for garnish.*

$1/2$ cup (2 oz/60 g) raspberries

$1/2$ cup (2 oz/60 g) blueberries

$1/2$ small apple, cored and cut into pieces

$1/2$ cup (4 oz/125 g) plain yogurt

about $1 1/2$ teaspoons sugar, or as needed

In an extractor, juice the raspberries, blueberries, and apple, in
that order. It may be necessary to open the machine and push
any remaining purée through the spout.

Stir in the yogurt. Taste for sweetness, adding the sugar if
needed. Stir again and serve. ✳

18

Carroty Vegetable Juice

SERVES 1

It would be hard to find a drink with a better nutritional profile.

$^1/_2$ small bunch spinach, well rinsed

3 carrots, scrubbed clean and cut into pieces

$^1/_2$ parsnip, peeled and cut into pieces

In an extractor, juice the spinach, carrots, and parsnip, in that order. Stir and serve. ✳

Mixed-Fruit Sunrise

SERVES 2

The grenadine will sink to create a beautiful red layer at the bottom of the glass. For a more adult drink, stir in a little tequila before you add the grenadine.

$1/2$ papaya, seeded, peeled, and cut into pieces

$1/4$ small cantaloupe, seeded, peeled, and cut into pieces

$1/2$ orange, peeled, seeded, and cut into pieces

6 large strawberries, hulled

4 teaspoons grenadine

In an extractor, juice half of the papaya pieces and half of the cantaloupe pieces, in that order. Then juice the remaining papaya pieces followed by the remaining cantaloupe, the orange, and the strawberries. Stir well.

Pour into 2 tall glasses, dividing evenly. Pour 2 teaspoons of the grenadine into each glass and wait until the grenadine sinks to the bottom. Serve at once. ✳

21

Spinach-Honeydew Juice

SERVES 1 OR 2

If you are not planning to drink this right away, don't add the lime rind to the extractor, as it will make the juice bitter after an hour or two. Judging the ripeness of a honeydew is difficult. If possible, buy a halved melon, and look for one that smells sweet.

$1/2$ small bunch spinach, well rinsed

1 lime wedge, including rind (see note)

$1/4$ small honeydew melon, seeded, peeled, and cut into pieces

In an extractor, juice the spinach, lime, and melon, in that order. Stir and serve. ✳

Winter Tingle

SERVES 1 OR 2

This juice features fruits available year-round, making it a fine choice for months when the produce stands are at their barest. To give it a fresher, cooler flavor, add a sprig or two of mint to the extractor.

1 pear, cored and cut into pieces

$1/2$ grapefruit, peeled, seeded, and cut into pieces

$1/4$ pineapple, cored, peeled, and cut into pieces

In an extractor, juice the pear, grapefruit, and pineapple, in that order. Stir and serve. ✳

Tomato-Vegetable Juice

SERVES 1 OR 2

This vitamin-packed powerhouse tastes like a Virgin Mary.
For a spicier version, add a small piece of fresh, seeded
chili pepper to the extractor along with the bell pepper.
If you like, squeeze in a little lemon or lime juice to brighten
the flavor, and garnish with a celery stalk.

1/4 red bell pepper (capsicum), seeded and
cut into pieces

1/2 small bunch fresh parsley

1 small green (spring) onion, green tops only

2 fresh cilantro sprigs (fresh coriander) or
3 fresh basil leaves

1 ripe tomato, cut into pieces

1 large celery stalk, cut into pieces

1/8 teaspoon celery salt

pinch of cayenne pepper

24

In an extractor, juice the bell pepper, parsley, green onion,
cilantro, tomato, and celery stalk, in that order. Add the celery
salt and cayenne pepper. Stir well and serve. ✴

Watermelon Agua Fresca

SERVES 2

*This refreshing drink is perfect on a hot summer's day.
Don't worry about the watermelon seeds, as they will spin out
in the extractor. If you like, make the same drink with any
melon, berry, or citrus fruit, or with pineapple.*

2 cups (12 oz/375 g) peeled watermelon cubes

$^1/_2$ cup (4 fl oz/125 ml) water

1 tablespoon sugar

ice cubes

In an extractor, juice the watermelon cubes. You should have
$1^1/_2$ cups (12 fl oz/375 ml) juice. Add the water and sugar, stirring until the sugar dissolves.

Place ice cubes in 2 tall glasses. Pour in the watermelon juice,
dividing evenly. Serve at once. ✳

26

Citrus Iced Tea

SERVES 6

*If you like your tea quite strong, you will want to add
an extra tea bag or two to the pan. Tea drinkers
who like a very sweet drink will need to increase the amount
of sugar and/or honey, while those who eschew sweeteners
can leave them out entirely.*

5 cups (40 fl oz/1.25 l) water

3 black tea bags

1 orange

1 tangerine

$^1/_2$ lemon

$^1/_2$ lime

$^1/_3$ cup (3 oz/90 g) sugar

1 tablespoon honey

ice cubes

27

In a saucepan over high heat, bring the water to a boil. Remove
from the heat and add the tea bags. Let steep for 5 minutes,
pushing them down into the water occasionally. Lift out and
discard the tea bags.

Juice the orange, tangerine, lemon, and lime with a citrus juicer,
or peel them, remove the seeds, cut into pieces, and juice with
an extractor. (You should have $^3/_4$ cup/6 fl oz/180 ml juice.) Add
to the tea in the saucepan. Add the sugar and honey, stirring
well to dissolve. Pour the tea into a pitcher, cover, and chill well.

To serve, fill tall glasses with ice and pour in the tea, dividing
evenly. Serve at once. ✷

Limeade

SERVES 2

Nothing quenches the thirst like a tall glass of limeade.
The number of limes you will need depends upon their size
and the amount of juice each yields. You can substitute
lemons to make lemonade, adding a little more sugar if
necessary. For a nice touch, float slices of lime in the glasses.

2–6 limes

1 cup (8 fl oz/250 ml) water

3 tablespoons sugar, or as needed

ice

Juice enough limes with a citrus juicer, or peel and seed them, cut them into pieces, and juice with an extractor, to yield $^1/_2$ cup (4 fl oz/125 ml) juice.

In a pitcher, combine the lime juice, water, and sugar. Stir until the sugar is dissolved. Taste for sweetness, adding more sugar if needed. Serve over ice in tall glasses. ✳

28

Mixed-Fruit Sangria

SERVES 12–14

This nontraditional version of sangria combines fresh fruit juices with the wine. Be careful: it's so delicious, it is easy to lose track of how much you've drunk. You can float slices of any fresh fruit on top; peach, nectarine, or lime are nice alternatives to the apple and orange.

1 large peach, halved, pitted, and cut into pieces

3 small plums, halved, pitted, and cut into pieces

2 cups (8 oz/250 g) strawberries, hulled

2 bottles (3 cups/24 fl oz/750 ml each) dry red wine

1/4 cup orange liqueur such as triple sec or Cointreau

3/4 cup (6 oz/185 g) sugar

1 small apple, cored and sliced

1 orange, sliced

ice cubes

In an extractor, juice the peach, plums, and strawberries, in that order. Pour into a large punch bowl or pitcher.

Add the wine, liqueur, and sugar, stirring until the sugar dissolves. Float the apple and orange slices on top.

To serve, fill individual glasses with ice and pour in the sangria. Serve at once. ✳

Plum Delicious

SERVES 1 OR 2

Seek out ripe, juicy plums for this refreshing sweet-tart drink.

1 apple, cored and cut into pieces

1 plum, halved, pitted, and cut into pieces

1/2 cup (2 oz/60 g) strawberries, hulled

In an extractor, juice the apple, plum, and strawberries, in that order. Stir and serve. ✳

Green Juice

SERVES 1

This mild-tasting juice carries a good supply of B vitamins.
Add the greens in small batches so the juicer doesn't stall.
For a colorful touch, garnish with shredded beets.

4 small beet leaves, well rinsed

$1/2$ large bunch spinach, well rinsed

$1/2$ bunch fresh parsley

lemon or lime juice to taste

In an extractor, juice the beet leaves, spinach, and parsley, in that order. Add the lemon or lime juice. Stir and serve. ✷

Carrot-Ginger Snap

SERVES 1

The carrots in this thirst-quencher deliver a big dose
of beta-carotene. For an even higher nutritional dividend,
substitute fresh spinach for the parsley. You don't
really taste the ginger until after you've swallowed; then
you feel the tingle.

$1/2$ bunch fresh parsley

1 piece fresh ginger, $1/2$ inch (12 mm), peeled

4 carrots, scrubbed clean and cut into pieces

In an extractor, juice the parsley, ginger, and carrots, in that order. Stir and serve. ✷

Summertime Treat

SERVES 1 OR 2

You may use 2 peaches or 2 nectarines instead of 1 of each. Check the cantaloupe for ripeness: the blossom end should give slightly when pressed and the melon should smell fragrant.

1 small nectarine, pitted and cut into pieces

1 small peach, pitted and cut into pieces

¼ small cantaloupe, seeded, peeled, and
cut into pieces

In an extractor, juice the nectarine, peach, and cantaloupe, in that order. Stir and serve. ✳

Mango-Berry Morning

SERVES 1

Sweet, juicy, and soft when ripe, mangoes have a yellow and/or red hue and a heady perfume. If good mangoes are unavailable, substitute 2 or 3 ripe nectarines.

1 small mango

1 cup (4 oz/125 g) strawberries, hulled

1 orange, peeled, seeded, and cut into pieces

Cut off the flesh from each side of the large, flat pit of the mango to form 2 large pieces. Trim any remaining flesh from around the edge of the pit, then discard the pit. Using a knife, peel away and discard the skin.

In an extractor, juice the mango, strawberries, and orange, in that order. Stir and serve. ✳

Red Red Red Drink

*Sweet, ripe strawberries—deep red, fragrant, and bursting
with vitamin C—yield the best results in this refreshing
drink. If the strawberries are underripe and tart, use
a sweet apple such as a Golden Delicious to balance the flavor.
In addition to the color, the beet contributes natural sweetness
and a generous amount of the B vitamin folate, along with
vitamin C, magnesium, potassium, and iron.*

1 cup (4 oz/125 g) strawberries, hulled

1 apple, cored and cut into pieces

1 red beet, scrubbed clean, trimmed, and cut into pieces

In an extractor, juice the strawberries, apple, and beet, in that
order. Stir and serve. ✳

35

Blueberry Float

SERVES 1

I prefer to serve this float with sorbet or sherbet,
which enhances the delicate flavor of the blueberries, rather
than ice cream, which overwhelms the berry taste. If you
don't have any grenadine (a pomegranate-flavored syrup),
use honey instead.

1 cup (4 oz/125 g) blueberries

1 tablespoon grenadine

1/2 cup (4 fl oz/125 ml) club soda or seltzer

1 scoop mango sorbet

In an extractor, juice the blueberries. Stir in the grenadine and
the club soda or seltzer. Top with the sorbet. Serve at once. ✳

36

Banana-Strawberry Daiquiri

SERVES 2 OR 3

If you like the flavor of rum, you may want to add a little more, and if you like sweet drinks, you'll need more sugar, too. If you don't have the chance to chill the fruits before juicing, swirl the daiquiris over ice to chill them before serving. For a retro look, garnish each glass with a cocktail umbrella, tilting it off the rim. Otherwise, a whole strawberry or a lime slice makes a nice garnish.

1 small ripe banana, peeled, cut into pieces, and chilled

2 cups (8 oz/250 g) strawberries, hulled and chilled

1/2 lime, peeled, seeded, cut into pieces, and chilled

1/4 cup (2 fl oz/60 ml) rum

2 tablespoons sugar

In an extractor, juice the banana, strawberries, and lime, in that order. Add the rum and sugar, stirring until the sugar dissolves.

To serve, pour into individual glasses. Serve at once. ✳

37

SOUPS AND SALADS

Chilled Tropical Soup

SERVES 2

*If preferred, chill the fruits before juicing, then serve this smooth
dessert soup straight from the extractor in chilled bowls. For
a lovely addition, float slices of kiwifruit on top of each serving.*

1/2 banana, peeled and cut into pieces

2 small kiwifruits, peeled and cut into pieces

1/4 pineapple, cored, peeled, and cut into pieces

2 oranges, peeled, seeded, and cut into pieces

1 tablespoon rum (optional)

In an extractor, juice the banana, kiwifruits, pineapple, and
oranges, in that order. Stir in the rum, if desired. Cover and
chill. Stir again before serving in chilled bowls. ✻

Onion Soup

SERVES 4–6

Serve this full-flavored soup as is, or spoon it into heatproof crocks, float a slice of toasted crusty French bread in each bowl, and top with a generous amount of shredded Gruyère cheese. Just before serving, broil until the cheese is melted and browned.

2 tablespoons unsalted butter

2 large yellow onions, thinly sliced

$\frac{1}{2}$ teaspoon dried thyme

1$\frac{1}{4}$ lb (625 g) white mushrooms, brushed clean

1 portobello mushroom, brushed clean and cut into pieces

2 large celery stalks, cut into pieces

1 parsnip, peeled and cut into pieces

1 large carrot, scrubbed clean and cut into pieces

1$\frac{1}{2}$ cups (12 fl oz/375 ml) beef or vegetable broth or Vegetable Stock (page 43)

1 cup (8 fl oz/250 ml) water

$\frac{1}{4}$ cup (2 fl oz/60 ml) dry red wine

2 bay leaves

salt and ground pepper to taste

42

In a large, heavy saucepan over medium-high heat, melt the butter. Add the onions and thyme and cook, stirring, until softened, about 5 minutes. Reduce the heat to low, cover, and cook for 10 minutes. Uncover and continue to cook, stirring occasionally, until golden, 30–40 minutes longer.

Meanwhile, in an extractor, juice the mushrooms, celery, parsnip, and carrot, in that order. You may have to stop once or twice to discard the pulp from the machine.

Add the juice, broth or stock, water, wine, and bay leaves to the onions. Bring to a boil over medium-high heat, then reduce the heat to medium-low and simmer, uncovered, until the flavors are blended, about 20 minutes. Discard the bay leaves. Season with salt and pepper, then serve. ✳

Vegetable Stock

MAKES ABOUT 5 CUPS (40 FL OZ/1.25 L)

A juicer is ideal for making a truly tasty vegetable stock.
The ingredient amounts are flexible, and other mild-
tasting vegetables such as celery root (celeriac), parsley root,
kohlrabi, or turnip may be added or substituted.
Use this stock in cooking, or as a pick-me-up in
the middle of the afternoon.

1/2 bunch fresh parsley

1/2 tomato, cut into pieces

3 carrots, scrubbed clean and cut into pieces

3 large celery stalks, cut into pieces

1 parsnip, peeled and cut into pieces

4 cups (32 fl oz/1 l) water

1 small leek

1/2 small bunch fresh dill

salt and ground pepper to taste

43

In an extractor, juice the parsley, tomato, carrots, celery, and parsnip, in that order. Reserve the pulp.

In a large saucepan over high heat, combine the juice, water, leek, dill, and the reserved pulp. Bring to a boil, then reduce the heat to medium-low and simmer, uncovered, until the flavors are blended, about 30 minutes.

Strain the stock through a fine-mesh sieve into a large bowl. Using the back of a large spoon, press any liquid from the pulp mixture into the bowl. Discard the leftover pulp mixture. Season with salt and pepper. Use immediately, or transfer to an airtight container and refrigerate for up to 5 days. ✳

15-Minute Carrot and Parsnip Soup

SERVES 4

You could substitute celeriac (celery root) or fennel for the parsnips and still have an incredibly delicious soup. Serve piping hot to fend off the chill of winter.

5 large carrots, well scrubbed and cut into pieces

2 parsnips, well scrubbed and cut into pieces

1 small leek, white part only

3 tablespoons butter

$1/4$ cup ($1 1/2$ oz/45 g) all-purpose (plain) flour

$1 1/2$ cups (12 fl oz/375 ml) chicken broth

$1/2$ cup (4 fl oz/125 ml) heavy (double) cream

$1/2$ teaspoon salt

$1/8$ teaspoon ground nutmeg

45

In an extractor, juice the carrots, parsnips, and leek, in that order (you may have to stop the juicer to remove the pulp). You should have 2 cups (16 fl oz/500 ml) juice.

In a saucepan over medium-high heat, melt the butter. Add the flour, stirring, until absorbed, about 30 seconds. Stir in the carrot-parsnip juice, broth, and cream. Cook, stirring, until the mixture comes to a boil. Stir in the salt and nutmeg. Ladle into warmed individual bowls and serve immediately. ✳

Pear, Blood Orange, and Endive Salad with Papaya Dressing

SERVES 4

Here, an aromatic dressing complements a simple mix of bitter greens. Use a coral-fleshed papaya for a prettier color and sweeter flavor. If blood oranges are unavailable, use regular oranges.

FOR THE DRESSING

¹/₂ papaya, seeded, peeled, and cut into pieces

2 tablespoons olive oil

2 tablespoons red wine vinegar

I tablespoon mayonnaise

FOR THE SALAD

2 blood oranges

I bunch arugula (rocket), stemmed

2 Belgian endives (chicory/witloof), cored, separated into leaves, and cut into bite-sized pieces

I small pear, cored and thinly sliced

3 tablespoons walnut pieces

46

To make the dressing, in an extractor, juice the papaya (you may have to open the juicer to push the purée through). In a bowl, combine the papaya purée, olive oil, vinegar, and mayonnaise. Stir until smooth.

To make the salad, using a sharp knife, cut a slice off the top and bottom of each orange to expose the fruit. Slice off the rind in thick strips, cutting around the contour of the orange to expose the flesh. Holding the orange over a bowl, cut along either side of each section, letting the sections drop into the bowl. Remove any seeds and discard.

In a large bowl, combine the arugula and endive. Arrange on 4 plates. Divide the orange segments, pear, and walnuts evenly among the plates. Drizzle the dressing on top and serve. ✳

Green Salad with Beet Red Dressing

SERVES 8

Mesclun is the Provençal term for a mix of young, tender salad greens. If you can't find mesclun or a similar potpourri, you can substitute red or green leaf lettuce.

FOR THE DRESSING

1 small red beet, about 3 oz (90 g), scrubbed clean, trimmed, and cut into pieces

1 tablespoon honey mustard

1 teaspoon red wine vinegar

3 tablespoons olive oil

FOR THE SALAD

$^{1}/_{2}$ cup (2 oz/60 g) walnuts

$^{1}/_{4}$ lb (125 g) mesclun (see note)

1 bunch watercress, tough stems removed

1 large Belgian endive (chicory/witloof), cored, separated into leaves, and cut into bite-sized pieces

1 red (Spanish) onion, thinly sliced

1 tart apple, quartered, cored, and sliced

3 tablespoons raisins

$^{1}/_{2}$ cup (2$^{1}/_{2}$ oz/75 g) crumbled Roquefort cheese

In an extractor, juice the beet (you should have $^{1}/_{4}$ cup/2 fl oz/ 60 ml juice). Place in a small bowl, stir in the honey mustard and vinegar, and then whisk in the oil. Set aside.

To make the salad, preheat an oven to 350°F (180°C). Spread the walnuts on a baking sheet and toast until they begin to color and are fragrant, 8–10 minutes. Pour onto a small plate and let cool.

In a large bowl, toss together the mesclun, watercress, endive, and onion. Drizzle the dressing over the greens and toss to coat well. Divide evenly among individual plates. Top each serving with an equal amount of the walnuts, apple, raisins, and cheese. Serve at once. ✳

Tomato-Orange Soup

SERVES 4

*Attempt this soup only when ripe, good-tasting tomatoes
are in the market. Don't be put off by the unusual combination
of flavors here. It works. Add a little cayenne pepper
with the salt for an extra bite.*

3 or 4 oranges

2 or 3 ripe tomatoes, cut into pieces

1 tablespoon butter

$^1/_2$ cup (1$^1/_2$ oz/45 g) thinly sliced leek,
including light green tops

1$^1/_2$ cups (12 fl oz/375 ml) chicken broth or
Vegetable Stock (page 43)

2 tablespoons brown sugar

1 tablespoon chopped fresh cilantro (fresh coriander)

$^1/_4$ teaspoon ground ginger

$^1/_4$ teaspoon salt

49

Finely grate the zest from 1 orange and reserve.

Peel and seed all the oranges and cut them into pieces. In an extractor, juice the oranges (you should have 1 cup/8 fl oz/250 ml
juice) and then the tomatoes (you should have 2 cups/16 fl oz/
500 ml juice).

In a saucepan over medium-high heat, melt the butter. Add the
leek and cook, stirring, until softened, about 2 minutes. Stir in
the orange and tomato juices, the broth or stock, brown sugar,
cilantro, ginger, $^1/_4$ teaspoon of the orange zest, and the salt.
Bring to a boil, then reduce the heat to low and simmer, uncovered, for 5 minutes to blend the flavors.

Ladle into warmed bowls and serve at once. ✳

Lentil Salad with Citrus Dressing

SERVES 2–4

Studding the onion with the cloves makes removing both of these flavor enhancers easy once the lentils are cooked. For a nice presentation, serve the salad on a bed of lettuce leaves as a main course or as an accompaniment to grilled chicken.

FOR THE LENTILS

4 cups (32 fl oz/1 l) water

1 small yellow onion

6 whole cloves

1 cup (7 oz/220 g) lentils

FOR THE DRESSING

1/2 orange, or more as needed

1/2 small lemon

3 tablespoons olive oil

1 teaspoon Dijon mustard

1/2 clove garlic, minced

1 teaspoon salt

1/4 teaspoon pepper

2 or 3 large celery stalks, chopped

1/2 large red bell pepper (capsicum), chopped

1/2 small red (Spanish) onion, chopped

lettuce leaves for serving

50

To prepare the lentils, in a large saucepan, bring the water to a boil. Stud the onion with the cloves, then add the onion and lentils to the saucepan. Return to a boil, then reduce the heat to medium-low and simmer, uncovered, until the lentils are tender but still whole, 20–30 minutes. Drain and discard the onion. Let cool.

To make the dressing, grate the zest of the orange to make
$1/2$ teaspoon; set aside. Juice the orange and lemon with a citrus
juicer, or peel and seed them, cut them into pieces, and juice
with an extractor. In a small bowl, stir together the orange and
lemon juice, the olive oil, mustard, orange zest, garlic, salt, and
pepper. You should have $1/2$ cup (4 fl oz/125 ml) dressing; if you
have less, add more orange juice.

To assemble the salad, in a large bowl, toss the lentils with the
celery, red pepper, and onion. Add the dressing and toss to
coat. Serve the salad on a bed of lettuce leaves. ✳

Lemon-Spinach Soup

SERVES 4

The juice of a lemon makes this fragrant green soup tart
and flavorful. You may want to begin by adding only
2 tablespoons lemon juice, and then add more to your taste.
Accompany with a loaf of crusty bread or breadsticks.

1 lemon

3 cups (24 fl oz/750 ml) chicken broth

1 cup (8 fl oz/250 ml) water

1/2 small bunch fresh flat-leaf (Italian) parsley, chopped

1/2 small bunch fresh dill, chopped

3 tablespoons orzo or other small dried pasta

1 small bunch fresh spinach, well rinsed and
coarsely chopped

52

Juice the lemon with a citrus juicer, or peel it, remove the
seeds, and juice with an extractor. You should have about
3 tablespoons juice.

In a saucepan over high heat, combine the broth, water, and
lemon juice. Bring to a boil, then add the parsley, dill, and
pasta. Return to a boil, then reduce the heat to medium-low
and simmer, uncovered, for about 8 minutes. Add the spinach
and continue to simmer until the spinach is wilted and tender,
2–3 minutes longer.

Serve in warmed individual bowls. ✳

MAIN COURSES

Tomato-Basil Risotto

*To ensure a creamy result, use Arborio rice, a
medium-grain Italian variety available in most markets and
in specialty-food shops. If you like, garnish with sprigs of
fresh basil and accompany with breadsticks.*

2–4 ripe tomatoes, cut into pieces

2 cups (16 fl oz/500 ml) Vegetable Stock (page 43)
or chicken broth

2 tablespoons olive oil

1/4 cup (1 1/4 oz/37 g) finely chopped yellow onion

1 cup (7 oz/220 g) Arborio rice

1/2 cup (2 oz/60 g) grated Parmesan cheese,
plus extra for garnish

1/4 cup (1/3 oz/10 g) chopped fresh basil

In an extractor, juice enough tomatoes to yield about 2 cups
(16 fl oz/500 ml) juice. In a saucepan over low heat, combine
the juice and stock or broth. Bring to a simmer. Adjust the heat
to maintain a gentle simmer while you make the risotto.

In a large, heavy saucepan over medium heat, warm the olive
oil. Add the onion and cook, stirring, for 1 minute. Add the rice
and cook, stirring, until coated with the oil, about 1 minute. Add
1/2 cup (4 fl oz/125 ml) of the hot stock mixture to the rice and
cook, stirring constantly, until the rice has absorbed the liquid
and a clear path forms on the bottom of the pot as you stir. Re-
peat, adding liquid a little at a time and stirring continuously,
until the risotto is creamy and the rice is al dente (tender but
firm to the bite). Total cooking time after the first addition of
the liquid is 20–30 minutes. Stir in the cheese and basil.

Divide the risotto among warmed individual bowls, top with a
sprinkling of grated cheese, and serve at once. ✳

Roast Pork Tenderloin with Bing Cherry Sauce

SERVES 4–6

1 tablespoon coriander seeds

2 cloves garlic, minced

1 teaspoon salt

$^1/_2$ teaspoon ground pepper

1 pork tenderloin, 2–2$^1/_2$ lb (1–1.25 kg)

1$^1/_2$ lb (750 g) Bing cherries, pitted

2 tablespoons sugar

1 tablespoon cornstarch (cornflour)

2 teaspoons lemon juice

$^1/_4$ teaspoon ground coriander

$^1/_8$ teaspoon salt

58

Preheat an oven to 350°F (180°C).

Place the coriander seeds in a sturdy plastic bag. Using a meat mallet or other heavy object, crush into little pieces. In a small bowl, stir together the crushed seeds, garlic, salt, and pepper. Rub the mixture over the entire surface of the pork. Place the pork in a 9-by-13-inch (23-by-33-cm) baking pan.

Roast until an instant-read thermometer inserted into the thickest part of the pork registers 170°F (77°C), or until the center of the roast is no longer pink when cut into with a knife, about 1 hour and 20 minutes.

Meanwhile, in an extractor, juice the cherries; you should have 1$^1/_2$ cups (12 fl oz/375 ml) juice. Stir in the sugar, cornstarch, lemon juice, ground coriander, and salt, mixing well.

When the pork is ready, transfer it to a cutting board and tent loosely with aluminum foil. Place the baking pan on the stove top over high heat. Pour in the juice mixture, bring to a boil, and deglaze the pan, stirring with a wooden spoon to remove any browned bits from the pan bottom. Remove from the heat.

Slice the roast and arrange the slices on a warmed platter. Pour the sauce into a bowl and pass at the table. ✳

Mushroom-Vegetable Quiche

This quiche has a lumpy-bumpy top, but the taste is just great. If you don't feel like making your own pie crust, use a purchased one, but be sure it is a deep-dish crust.

FOR THE PASTRY

1 1/2 cups (7 1/2 oz/235 g) all-purpose (plain) flour

1 teaspoon salt

3/4 cup (6 oz/185 g) vegetable shortening

4 or 5 tablespoons (2–2 1/2 fl oz/60–80 ml) ice water

FOR THE FILLING

1 large carrot, scrubbed clean and cut into pieces

1 large celery stalk, cut into pieces

1 small red bell pepper (capsicum), seeded and cut into pieces

1 small yellow onion, cut into pieces

1 1/2 tablespoons unsalted butter or margarine

3 1/2 cups (10 1/2 oz/330 g) sliced fresh mushrooms

3 eggs

2 cups (10 oz/315 g) shredded zucchini

1/2 cup (4 fl oz/125 ml) milk

1/2 teaspoon dried tarragon

1 teaspoon salt, or to taste

1/4 teaspoon ground pepper

1 1/2 cups (6 oz/185 g) shredded Jarlsberg cheese

Preheat an oven to 400°F (200°C).

To make the pastry, in a bowl, stir together the flour and the salt. Add the shortening and, using a pastry blender or 2 knives, cut it in until the mixture resembles coarse cornmeal.

Add the ice water, 1 tablespoon at a time, and stir and toss with a fork just until the mixture holds together. Form into a ball, then flatten into a disk.

On a lightly floured work surface, roll out the dough into a round 11 inches (28 cm) in diameter. Drape the dough over the rolling pin and carefully transfer it to a 9-inch (23-cm) deep-dish pie dish. Gently ease the pastry into the dish. Fold the edges under and crimp attractively. Line with parchment (baking) paper or aluminum foil and fill with pie weights or dried beans.

Bake until set and lightly golden but not browned, about 10 minutes. Remove from the oven and place on a rack. Remove the weights and paper or foil. Let cool. Reduce the oven temperature to 350°F (180°C).

To make the filling, in an extractor, juice the carrot, celery, bell pepper, and onion, in that order. Reserve the pulp. In a frying pan over medium-high heat, melt the butter or margarine. Add the mushrooms and cook, stirring, until softened, about 4 minutes. Remove from the heat.

61

In a large bowl, whisk the eggs until lightly blended. Add the juice and pulp from the juicer, the zucchini, milk, tarragon, salt, and pepper. Whisk until combined. Stir in the mushrooms and the cheese. Pour into the pie shell.

Bake until puffy and slightly browned on top, about 45 minutes. Transfer to a rack and let cool for 10 minutes before slicing. ✳

Cornish Hens with Tangerine-Honey Sauce

SERVES 2–4

Tangerines can be found in markets most of the year. During those months when they are unavailable, you can prepare this dish using oranges. Add 1 or 2 tablespoons of orange liqueur to the juice to enhance the flavor of the sauce.

2 Cornish hens, about 1 ½ lb (750 g) each

salt and ground pepper to taste

3 tangerines

3 tablespoons honey

1 teaspoon soy sauce

1 clove garlic, minced

Preheat an oven to 350°F (180°C).

Rinse the game hens and pat dry. Sprinkle lightly inside and out with salt and pepper.

Grate the zest of 1 tangerine (you should have 1 teaspoon grated zest), then thinly slice the tangerine. Using your fingertips, gently loosen the skin on the breast of each game hen, being careful not to tear the skin. Slip 1 or 2 tangerine slices between the skin and flesh of each bird. Place half of the remaining slices into the cavity of each hen. Place the hens in a 9-inch (23-cm) square baking pan.

Juice the remaining 2 tangerines with a citrus juicer, or peel and seed them, cut them into pieces, and juice with an extractor. You should have about ½ cup (4 fl oz/125 ml) juice. Stir in the honey, soy sauce, tangerine zest, and garlic to form a basting sauce.

Pour the tangerine mixture over the hens. Roast, basting 3 or 4 times with the pan juices, until an instant-read thermometer inserted into a thigh away from the bone registers 170°F (77°C), or the juices run clear when a thigh is pierced, 1¼–1½ hours.

Remove from the oven and serve. Pour the pan juices into a warmed bowl and pass at the table. ✳

63

Chicken Breasts with Brandied Plum Sauce

SERVES 4

This recipe works well with any tart fruit juice, such as strawberry or apricot. Accompany with a mixture of white and wild rices to soak up the extra sauce.

FOR THE SAUCE

3–5 ripe plums, halved, pitted, and cut into pieces

2 tablespoons firmly packed brown sugar

1/4 teaspoon ground nutmeg or cloves

1/4 teaspoon salt, or to taste

FOR THE CHICKEN

4 skinless, boneless chicken breast halves, about 6 oz (185 g) each

salt and ground pepper to taste

2 tablespoons all-purpose (plain) flour

2 ripe plums, halved and pitted

1 tablespoon unsalted butter

1 tablespoon vegetable oil

3 tablespoons brandy

To make the sauce, in an extractor, juice the plums. You should have about 1 1/2 cups (12 fl oz/375 ml) juice. Pour the plum juice into a small bowl and stir in the brown sugar, nutmeg or cloves, and salt. Set aside.

To prepare the chicken, place each breast between 2 pieces of waxed paper. Using a meat pounder, pound the breasts to an even thickness. Lightly season each breast with salt and pepper. Pour the flour onto a piece of waxed paper, then lightly dredge the chicken breasts in it. Set aside.

Cut each plum half into 3 or 4 wedges. In a large frying pan over medium-high heat, melt the butter. Add the plum wedges and cook, stirring, until slightly softened, about 2 minutes. Remove the plums from the pan.

In the same pan over medium-high heat, warm the oil. Add the chicken breasts and cook, turning once, until lightly browned and no longer pink in the center, 2–3 minutes on each side. Remove the chicken from the pan and remove the pan from the heat. Pour in the brandy and deglaze the pan, stirring to dislodge any browned bits from the pan bottom.

Return the chicken and plums to the pan and pour in the sauce. Warm gently over medium-high heat until just heated through, 1–2 minutes. Divide among warmed individual plates and serve at once. ✳

65

Pot Roast Simmered in Vegetable Juices with Dumplings

SERVES 8

Any one of a number of different cuts of meat can be used to make this pot roast, including bottom round, top round, chuck roast, or brisket. Just be sure to cook the meat long enough for it to become tender. Add the dumplings to the pot roast just a few minutes before serving.

3 celery stalks, cut into pieces

2 carrots, scrubbed clean and cut into pieces

2 ripe tomatoes, cut into pieces

1 parsnip, peeled and cut into pieces

1 yellow onion, cut into pieces

1 tablespoon cider vinegar

$1/2$ teaspoon Worcestershire sauce

$1/4$ teaspoon hot-pepper sauce

1 tablespoon vegetable oil

1 beef pot roast, about 4 lb (2 kg) (see note)

3 cups (24 fl oz/750 ml) water

1 teaspoon salt

FOR THE DUMPLINGS

4 eggs

3 tablespoons chopped fresh parsley

$1 1/2$ cups ($7 1/2$ oz/235 g) all-purpose (plain) flour

2 tablespoons vegetable oil

1 teaspoon salt

In an extractor, juice the celery, carrots, tomatoes, parsnip, and onion, in that order. Stir in the vinegar, Worcestershire sauce, and hot-pepper sauce.

66

In a dutch oven or other large, heavy pot over high heat, warm the oil. Add the roast and, turning as necessary, brown well on all sides, about 4 minutes total. Pour in the vegetable juice and water and bring to a boil. Reduce the heat to low, cover, and simmer for 1 hour. Uncover and continue to simmer until the meat is nearly tender when pierced with a fork, 1–2 hours longer depending on the cut. Add the salt and continue to simmer, uncovered, until the meat is tender, about 30 minutes longer.

About 20 minutes before the roast is ready, make the dumplings: In a bowl, beat the eggs with the parsley until blended. Add the flour, oil, and salt and stir until well combined. The mixture should have the texture of soft bread dough. Bring a large saucepan three-fourths full of salted water to a rapid boil. Drop the dumpling dough by rounded teaspoonfuls into the water and cook over high heat until the dumplings rise to the surface and look fluffy, 3–4 minutes. To test for doneness, remove a dumpling from the pot and cut into it with a knife. It should be firm throughout.

Using a slotted spoon, transfer the dumplings (you should have 24–30) to the pot in which the roast is simmering. Leave for a few minutes so the dumplings absorb flavor from the gravy.

To serve, remove the roast from the pan and place on a warmed platter. Carve across the grain into slices. Using a slotted spoon, lift the dumplings from the pan and arrange alongside. Pour the gravy into a bowl and pass at the table. ✳

Grilled Lamb with Blackberry-Mustard Marinade

SERVES 4

*The combination of fruit, mustard, and herbs makes a
spicy-sweet marinade for butterflied leg of lamb. Raspberries
may be substituted for the blackberries.*

FOR THE MARINADE

1³/₄ cups (7 oz/220 g) blackberries

2 tablespoons olive oil

2 tablespoons firmly packed brown sugar

1 tablespoon Dijon mustard

¹/₂ teaspoon salt

¹/₄ teaspoon dried thyme

¹/₄ teaspoon ground pepper

3 cloves garlic, minced

¹/₂ leg of lamb (shank end), boned and butterflied
(about 4¹/₂ lb/2.25 kg before boning)

To make the marinade, in an extractor, juice the blackberries.
You should have about ¹/₂ cup (4 fl oz/125 ml) juice. In a large
nonreactive baking dish, whisk together the blackberry juice,
olive oil, brown sugar, mustard, salt, thyme, pepper, and garlic.
Add the lamb and turn to coat. Let marinate for 20 minutes,
turning once.

Meanwhile, prepare a fire in a grill or preheat a broiler (griller).

Remove the lamb from the marinade and discard the marinade.
Place the lamb on the grill rack or broiler pan about 6 inches
(15 cm) from the heat source. Grill or broil, turning once, until
the meat is browned on the outside and deep pink in the center
when cut into with a sharp knife, 18–20 minutes on each side
for medium-rare, or until done to your liking.

Let stand for 5 minutes before carving. Carve across the grain
into thin slices to serve. ✳

Spicy Grilled Shrimp with Avocado Mousse

SERVES 4

Quickly prepared with the aid of a juice extractor, the ultrasmooth avocado mousse also makes a delicious dip for raw vegetables or tortilla chips. Omit the cayenne pepper if you don't like your food too spicy.

FOR THE SHRIMP

2 tablespoons olive oil

1 teaspoon chili powder

1/2 teaspoon ground black pepper

1/4 teaspoon ground cumin

1/4 teaspoon salt

1/8 teaspoon cayenne pepper

1 1/2 lb (750 g) jumbo shrimp (prawns), peeled and deveined

FOR THE MOUSSE

1 small ripe avocado, pitted, peeled, and cut into pieces

1 clove garlic

1/2 lime

1/4 cup (2 oz/60 g) mayonnaise

1/4 cup (2 oz/60 g) plain yogurt

1 tablespoon chopped fresh cilantro (fresh coriander)

To cook the shrimp, prepare a fire in a grill and position the grill rack 4–6 inches (10–15 cm) from the fire. Alternatively, preheat a broiler (griller). If using wooden skewers, soak 8 skewers in warm water for 15 minutes.

In a bowl, combine the olive oil, chili powder, black pepper, cumin, salt, and cayenne pepper. Add the shrimp and turn to coat. Let marinate for 10 minutes.

Meanwhile, make the mousse: Using an extractor, purée the avocado, then juice the garlic. Peel the lime half, remove the seeds, and juice the fruit. Combine the avocado purée and lime and garlic juices in a small bowl. Add the mayonnaise, yogurt, and cilantro. Stir until well combined.

Drain the skewers and thread the shrimp onto them. Place the skewers on the grill rack or on a broiler (griller) pan. Grill or broil, turning once, until evenly pink, 1–2 minutes on each side. Set aside.

To serve, arrange the skewers on a platter and pass the mousse alongside. ✳

71

Orange Beef

SERVES 4

2 tablespoons soy sauce

1 1/2 tablespoons cornstarch (cornflour)

2 tablespoons mirin or dry sherry

2 tablespoons sugar

1 1/2 lb (750 g) beef steak such as London broil,
flank steak, or other tender cut, cut against the grain into
slices 1/4 inch (6 mm) thick

1 orange

1/4 cup (2 fl oz/60 ml) vegetable oil

1 tablespoon peeled and minced fresh ginger

3 cloves garlic, minced

3 green onions, including the tender green tops,
cut into 2-inch (5-cm) lengths

1 teaspoon Asian sesame oil

72

In a bowl, stir together 1 tablespoon each of the soy sauce, corn-starch, wine, and sugar. Add the beef and toss to coat evenly. Let stand for 10 minutes.

Meanwhile, using a vegetable peeler, remove the zest from the orange in long, narrow strips. Juice the orange with a citrus juicer, or peel and seed, cut into pieces, and juice with an extrac-tor. You should have 1/2 cup (4 fl oz/125 ml) juice. Add the zest, the remaining 1 tablespoon soy sauce, 1/2 tablespoon cornstarch, 1 tablespoon wine, and 1 tablespoon sugar. Stir well.

In a wok or large, deep frying pan over high heat, warm the veg-etable oil. When it is hot, add half of the beef mixture and stir and toss until the meat is no longer pink on the outside, 2–3 minutes. Using a slotted spoon, transfer the beef to a plate. Re-peat with the remaining beef. Discard the oil from the pan.

Return the pan to high heat. Add the ginger, garlic, green onions, and sesame oil and stir and toss until softened, about 1 minute. Quickly stir the orange juice mixture and then add to the pan. Cook, stirring, until thickened, about 2 minutes. Stir in the beef and heat through, about 2 minutes longer. Transfer to a warmed serving dish and serve at once. ✳

Seared Pepper Tuna with Grapefruit-Cilantro Sauce

SERVES 4

3 grapefruits

2 tablespoons chopped fresh cilantro (fresh coriander)

I teaspoon peeled and minced fresh ginger

2 tuna steaks, each about I lb (500 g) and
I inch (2.5 cm) thick

salt to taste

2 teaspoons ground pepper

I tablespoon butter

73

Grate enough of the zest from 1 of the grapefruits to measure 1 teaspoon, then juice the grapefruit with a citrus juicer, or peel and seed it, cut it into pieces, and juice with an extractor. You should have about 1 cup (8 fl oz/250 ml) juice. Stir in the zest, cilantro, and ginger. Set aside.

Using a small, sharp knife, cut a slice off the top and the bottom of the remaining 2 grapefruits. Place each grapefruit upright on a cutting board and thickly slice off the peel in strips, cutting around the contour of the fruit to expose the flesh. Holding the fruit over a bowl, cut along either side of each section to free it from the membrane, letting the sections drop into the bowl. Remove any seeds and discard. Set aside.

Cut each tuna steak into 2 equal pieces. Season the tuna with salt. Spread the ground pepper on a plate. Roll the entire edge of each piece of tuna in the pepper to coat evenly.

In a large frying pan over medium-high heat, melt the butter. Add the tuna steaks and cook, turning once, for 2 minutes on each side for rare, 3–4 minutes on each side for medium-rare, or 4–5 minutes on each side for well done. Transfer to a warmed platter or individual plates and keep warm.

Return the pan to high heat. Add the juice-cilantro mixture and the grapefruit sections and cook, stirring, until the mixture comes to a boil, 2–3 minutes. Boil until the liquid is reduced by half and the grapefruit sections have disintegrated, 2–3 minutes. Spoon the sauce over the tuna and serve immediately. ✳

Mango Chicken Curry

SERVES 4–6

*Thick fresh mango purée adds tantalizing sweetness and
body to this curry. If the round, flat Indian breads such as
paratha or nan are available in your area, they are
an ideal accompaniment. Warmed pita bread is a good
substitute. Serve with rice pilaf.*

$^{1}/_{2}$ ripe mango

2 tablespoons vegetable oil

1 $^{1}/_{2}$ cups (7 $^{1}/_{2}$ oz/235 g) chopped yellow onion

1 tablespoon minced fresh ginger

3 cloves garlic, minced

1 $^{1}/_{2}$ tablespoons curry powder

1 chicken, about 4 $^{1}/_{2}$ lb (2.25 kg), cut into pieces

1 cup (8 fl oz/250 ml) water

1 tablespoon lemon juice

1 teaspoon salt

2 tablespoons chopped fresh cilantro (fresh coriander)

74

Cut off the flesh from one side of the large, flat pit of the mango.
Using a knife, peel away and discard the skin. Juice the flesh in
an extractor (you may have to open the juicer to push the purée
through).

In a large, heavy pot over medium-high heat, warm the oil. Add
the onion, ginger, and garlic and cook, stirring, until softened,
about 2 minutes. Stir in the curry powder. Add the chicken and
turn to coat with the curry mixture. Add the water, mango purée,
lemon juice, and salt. Bring to a boil, then reduce the heat to medium-low and simmer, uncovered, until the chicken is tender
and the juices run clear when a thigh is pierced with the tip of a
knife, about 40 minutes. Stir in the cilantro and serve. ✳

Grilled Vegetables with Red Pepper Aioli

SERVES 4

juice of 2 lemons

3 tablespoons olive oil

$^1/_4$ teaspoon each dried thyme and rosemary

1 clove garlic, minced

salt and ground black pepper to taste

1 zucchini (courgette) and 1 yellow summer squash, trimmed and cut lengthwise into slices $^1/_4$ inch (6 mm) thick

$^1/_2$ eggplant (aubergine), cut into slices $^1/_4$ inch (6 mm) thick

1 red bell pepper (capsicum), quartered and seeded

1 red (Spanish) onion, sliced $^1/_4$ inch (6 mm) thick

FOR THE RED PEPPER AIOLI

1 small red bell pepper (capsicum)

$^3/_4$ cup (6 fl oz/180 ml) mayonnaise

2 cloves garlic, minced

Pinch of cayenne pepper

Prepare a fire in a charcoal grill or preheat a broiler (griller).

In a large bowl, combine the lemon juice, olive oil, herbs, garlic, and salt and pepper. Add all the vegetables and toss to combine. Let stand for at least 10 minutes or for up to 4 hours.

Meanwhile, make the aioli: In an extractor, juice the red pepper. Pour into a small saucepan, bring to a boil, and cook uncovered, stirring frequently, until reduced to the consistency of tomato paste, about 3 minutes. Let cool.

In a small bowl, combine the mayonnaise, garlic, cayenne, and reduced pepper purée; mix well.

Remove the vegetables from the marinade, reserving the marinade. Place on a grill rack over a hot fire, or place on a broiler pan and slip under the broiler about 4 inches (10 cm) from the heat source. Grill or broil, brushing with the marinade and turning once, until browned and tender, 4–6 minutes total. Transfer the vegetables to a platter. Pass the aioli at the table. ✳

Salmon with Red Pepper and Fennel Sauce

SERVES 4

*Blackening spices, available in well-stocked food stores,
are a Cajun condiment first popularized outside of
Louisiana by acclaimed New Orleans chef Paul Prudhomme.
If you can't find blackening spices, substitute ³/₄ teaspoon
spicy seasoned salt and ¹/₄ teaspoon paprika.*

1 orange

1 red bell pepper (capsicum), seeded and cut into pieces

¹/₂ fennel bulb, trimmed, cored, and cut into pieces

3 tablespoons all-purpose (plain) flour

2 tablespoons butter, at room temperature

2 teaspoons blackening spices (see note)

4 salmon steaks, each 1 inch (2.5 cm) thick

1 tablespoon vegetable oil

¹/₄ teaspoon salt

¹/₈ teaspoon cayenne pepper

Grate the zest from the orange and set aside. Peel the orange, remove the seeds, and cut into pieces. In an extractor, juice the bell pepper, orange, and fennel, in that order. You should have about 1 cup (8 fl oz/250 ml) juice.

In a small bowl, mix together 1 tablespoon of the flour and 1 tablespoon of the butter; set aside. On a piece of waxed paper, stir together the remaining 2 tablespoons flour and the blackening spices. Dredge the salmon steaks in the flour-spice mixture, coating evenly.

In a large frying pan over medium-high heat, melt the remaining 1 tablespoon butter with the vegetable oil. Add the salmon steaks and cook, turning once, until opaque throughout, 2–3 minutes on each side for medium. Remove the salmon from the pan and keep warm.

Pour the juice into the pan and deglaze over medium-high heat, stirring to dislodge any browned bits from the pan bottom. Add the butter-flour mixture and continue to cook, stirring, until the mixture comes to a boil and thickens. Stir in the salt and cayenne pepper. Pour into a small warmed serving bowl.

To serve, divide the salmon among warmed individual plates. Pass the sauce at the table. ✳

DESSERTS

Poached Pears with Raspberry-Nectarine Sauce

SERVES 4

Peaches, nectarines, or even quinces can be used in place of the pears in this elegant recipe.

FOR THE PEARS

2–4 limes

5 cups (40 fl oz/1.25 l) water

³/₄ cup (6 oz/185 g) sugar

4 pears, peeled with stems intact

FOR THE SAUCE

2 nectarines, pitted and cut into pieces

1¹/₂ cups (6 oz/185 g) raspberries

1¹/₂ tablespoons sugar

¹/₂ teaspoon cornstarch (cornflour)

To prepare the pears, juice the limes with a citrus juicer, or peel and seed them and juice with an extractor. You should have about ¹/₂ cup (4 fl oz/125 ml) juice. In a large saucepan, combine the lime juice, water, and sugar and bring to a boil over medium-high heat.

Add the pears and return to a boil. Reduce the heat to medium-low and simmer, uncovered, until the pears are tender, 20–35 minutes, depending upon the ripeness of the pears. Using a slotted spoon, transfer the pears to a bowl. Reserve ¹/₄ cup (2 fl oz/60 ml) of the liquid for the sauce. Cover and chill the pears.

Meanwhile, prepare the sauce: Return the reserved poaching liquid to the saucepan. In an extractor, juice the nectarines and raspberries. Add the juice to the poaching liquid. In a small bowl, combine the sugar and cornstarch, then whisk into the sauce mixture. Bring to a boil over medium heat and cook, stirring constantly, until thickened, about 7 minutes. Let cool.

To serve, pour one-fourth of the sauce onto each individual plate and place a pear in the center. ✳

Raisin-Carrot Bundt Cake

SERVES 10–12

FOR THE CAKE

3 cups (15 oz/470 g) all-purpose (plain) flour

1 tablespoon ground cinnamon

2 teaspoons baking powder

1 teaspoon baking soda (bicarbonate of soda)

1/2 teaspoon salt

1 1/2 cups (9 oz/280 g) raisins

4 or 5 large carrots, scrubbed clean and cut into pieces

2 cups (1 lb/500 g) granulated sugar

1 cup (8 fl oz/250 ml) vegetable oil

1/4 cup (3 oz/90 g) light molasses

3 eggs

1 teaspoon vanilla extract (essence)

FOR THE ICING

1 cup (4 oz/125 g) confectioners' (icing) sugar

1 tablespoon orange juice

1/2 teaspoon grated orange zest

Preheat an oven to 350°F (180°C). Heavily butter and flour a 10-inch (25-cm) bundt pan, tapping out any excess flour.

To make the cake, in a large bowl, whisk together the flour, cinnamon, baking powder, baking soda, and salt. Stir in the raisins. In an extractor, juice the carrots, reserving the pulp. You should have about 1 cup (8 fl oz/250 ml) juice.

In a large bowl, using an electric mixer set on high speed, beat together the sugar, oil, molasses, and eggs until well combined. Stir in the carrot juice and pulp and the vanilla. Stir the flour mixture into the sugar mixture. Pour into the prepared pan.

Bake until a toothpick inserted into the center comes out clean, about 1 hour. Transfer to a rack, unmold, and let cool.

To make the icing, in a bowl, stir together the sugar and orange juice and zest. Drizzle over the cooled cake. ✳

Lemon Mousse

SERVES 4–6

*You may need as few as 2 or as many as 6 lemons for
this recipe, depending on their size and the amount of juice
they yield. If you like, serve the mousse with a
crispy cookie, and garnish with candied lemon peel.*

2–6 lemons (see note)

$^3/_4$ teaspoon unflavored gelatin

3 egg yolks

$^3/_4$ cup (6 oz/180 g) plus 2 tablespoons sugar

1 cup (8 fl oz/250 ml) heavy (double) cream

86

Grate the zest of 1 of the lemons and set aside. Juice enough
lemons with a citrus juicer, or peel and seed them and juice
with an extractor, to yield about $^1/_2$ cup (4 fl oz/125 ml) juice.
Place the juice in a small bowl and stir in the gelatin and grated
zest; let stand for 5 minutes.

In a heatproof bowl set over (not touching) barely simmering
water in a pan, lightly beat the egg yolks with a whisk. Whisk in
the $^3/_4$ cup (6 oz/180 g) sugar, $^1/_4$ cup (2 oz/60 g) at a time, and
then the lemon juice mixture. Cook, stirring with a wooden
spoon, until the mixture thickens enough to coat the back of the
spoon, 10–15 minutes. Remove from over the pan and refrigerate, stirring occasionally, until the mixture is thick enough to
hold its shape when dropped from the spoon, about 1 hour.

In a large bowl, beat the cream with the remaining 2 tablespoons sugar until stiff peaks form. Fold the lemon mixture
into the whipped cream. Spoon into 4–6 dessert glasses. Serve
immediately, or chill until serving. ✳

Carrot-Apple Muffins

MAKES 12 MUFFINS

*These muffins are not too sweet, which makes them
perfect with jam. Add an extra tablespoon of sugar if you
like your muffins sweeter or chopped walnuts
if you like them crunchy.*

$^3/_4$ cup (4 oz/125 g) all-purpose (plain) flour, sifted

1 tablespoon baking powder

1 teaspoon baking soda (bicarbonate of soda)

1 teaspoon ground cinnamon

$^1/_2$ teaspoon salt

2 carrots, scrubbed and cut into pieces

about $^2/_3$ cup (5 fl oz/160 ml) buttermilk

$^1/_3$ cup (3 oz/90 g) sugar

1 egg

3 tablespoons vegetable oil

3 tablespoons molasses

1 apple, peeled, cored, and chopped

Preheat an oven to 400°F (200°C). Butter twelve 2$^1/_2$-inch (6-cm) muffin cups.

In a bowl or on a piece of waxed paper, stir together the flour, baking powder, baking soda, cinnamon, and salt. In an extractor, juice the carrots, reserving the pulp. Add buttermilk to the carrot juice as needed to total 1 cup (8 fl oz/250 ml).

In a large bowl, beat together the buttermilk-juice mixture, carrot pulp, sugar, egg, vegetable oil, and molasses. Add the flour mixture and stir until combined but still lumpy. Stir in the apple. Spoon into the prepared muffin cups, dividing evenly; they will be full.

Bake until lightly browned on top, 22–25 minutes. Remove from the oven and turn out onto a rack to cool. ✳

Chocolate Roll with Raspberry Cream Filling

SERVES 8–10

Although this dessert has many steps, the final result is well worth the effort. Don't skip the chocolate glaze, as it adds a lovely richness to the cake. You can use just jelly or preserves in place of the cream filling, if desired.

FOR THE CAKE

confectioners' (icing) sugar for dusting towel

1 cup (4 oz/125 g) sifted all-purpose (plain) flour

$1/2$ cup (1 $1/2$ oz/45 g) unsweetened cocoa

1 teaspoon baking powder

4 eggs

1 cup (8 oz/250 g) sugar

$1/2$ cup (4 fl oz/125 ml) milk

$1/2$ teaspoon vanilla extract (essence)

FOR THE FILLING

1 cup (4 oz/125 g) raspberries

$1/2$ cup (3 oz/90 g) semisweet chocolate morsels

2 tablespoons unsalted butter

$3/4$ cup (6 fl oz/185 ml) heavy (double) cream

3 tablespoons sugar

FOR THE GLAZE

$1/2$ cup (3 oz/90 g) semisweet chocolate morsels

$1/3$ cup (3 fl oz/80 ml) heavy (double) cream

Preheat an oven to 375°F (190°C). Butter a 15$1/2$-by-10$1/2$-by-1-inch (39-by-26.5-by-2.5-cm) jelly-roll (Swiss roll) pan. Line the bottom with waxed paper and then butter and flour the paper well, tapping out any excess flour. Lay a clean kitchen towel slightly larger than the pan on a work surface and dust generously with confectioners' sugar.

In a bowl, sift together the sifted flour, cocoa, and baking powder. In a large bowl, using an electric mixer set on high speed, beat the eggs for 2 minutes. Add the sugar and beat for 3 minutes. Beat in the milk and vanilla until well blended. Stir in the flour mixture until smooth. Transfer the batter to the prepared pan, spreading evenly.

Bake until the cake pulls away from the sides of the pan, 15–20 minutes. Transfer to a rack and let cool for 3 minutes. Place the prepared towel, sugar side down, on top of the cake and carefully invert it onto a work surface. Lift off the pan and peel off the waxed paper. Beginning with a short edge and holding the towel against the cake, roll up the cake with the towel inside. Let the rolled cake cool on the rack.

While the cake is cooling, prepare the filling: In an extractor, juice the raspberries. Set aside 1 tablespoon juice for the glaze.

In the top pan of a double boiler or a heatproof bowl set over (not touching) simmering water, place the chocolate morsels and butter. Heat, stirring occasionally, just until melted and smooth. Remove from over the water and let cool.

In a large bowl, with the electric mixer on high speed, beat together the cream, sugar, and raspberry juice until firm peaks form. Fold in the melted chocolate just until no light streaks remain. Carefully unroll the cooled cake and remove the towel. Spread the filling evenly over the cake. Reroll the cake and place on a rack set inside a larger pan.

To make the glaze, in the top pan of the double boiler or a heatproof bowl set over (not touching) simmering water, place the chocolate morsels and cream. Heat, stirring occasionally, until the mixture is smooth and the chocolate has melted completely. Remove from over the water and stir in the reserved 1 tablespoon raspberry juice. Pour over the cake roll and spread to cover evenly. Chill well before serving.

To serve, transfer to a serving plate and cut into thin slices. ✳

Cantaloupe-Pineapple Granita

SERVES 4–6

*The Italian-style iced dessert known as a granita makes
excellent use of fresh fruit juices. The liqueur in this particular
recipe raises the freezing point so that the consistency remains
somewhat soft. Serve at the end of a grilled dinner eaten
outdoors at the height of summer. If you like, garnish with a
pineapple wheel or fresh orange slices.*

1/2 medium cantaloupe, seeded, peeled,
and cut into pieces

1/4 large pineapple, cored, peeled, and cut into pieces

2 tablespoons orange liqueur or orange juice

1 tablespoon sugar

In an extractor, juice the cantaloupe and then the pineapple;
stir to combine. Add the liqueur or orange juice and sugar and
stir until the sugar dissolves. Pour into a metal bowl and place
in the freezer for 2 hours.

Remove the mixture from the freezer and beat with an electric
mixer until no lumps or puddles of liquid remain. Return to
the freezer for 1 hour. Repeat 3 more times, or until the mixture
is completely frozen, beating every 1–2 hours, about 6–8 hours
total. The granita can be made up to 4 days ahead.

For a fluffy consistency, about 1 hour before serving, place the
frozen granita in a food processor and process just until the ice
crystals are broken up. Return to the freezer until ready to
serve. Serve in chilled dessert glasses. ✳

Mango Flan

SERVES 6

The sweet and tart flavor of the mango and orange give this custard a cool, refreshing character. Thin, crispy cookies are an ideal accompaniment.

$1/3$ cup (3 fl oz/80 ml) cold water

$1/2$ cup (4 oz/125 g) plus $1/3$ cup (3 oz/90 g) sugar

$1/2$ ripe mango, peeled and cut into pieces

$1/2$ orange, peeled, seeded, and cut into pieces

3 eggs

$3/4$ cup (6 fl oz/180 ml) milk

1 teaspoon vanilla extract (essence)

boiling water, as needed

93

Preheat an oven to 350°F (180°C). Butter six $3/4$-cup (6–fl oz/ 180-ml) custard cups.

In a small, heavy-bottomed saucepan over high heat, combine the cold water and the $1/2$ cup (4 oz/125 g) sugar. Bring to a boil, stirring just until the sugar dissolves. Continue to boil until the syrup starts to darken around the edges, 5–6 minutes. Then stir continuously and cook until the syrup turns a dark amber. Pour into the bottom of the prepared cups, dividing evenly. Place the cups in a roasting pan in which they fit without touching.

In an extractor, juice the mango and the orange, in that order (you may have to stop the juicer to push the purée through).

In a bowl, whisk the eggs until blended. Add the milk, the mango-orange juice, the remaining $1/3$ cup (3 oz/90 g) sugar, and the vanilla. Stir until just combined. (You don't want it to become too foamy.) Pour into the cups, dividing evenly. Pour boiling water into the roasting pan to a depth of 1 inch (2.5 cm).

Bake until a knife inserted into the center of a custard comes out clean, about 35 minutes. Remove from the oven, then re-move from the roasting pan. Let cool, then cover and chill.

To serve, run a thin-bladed knife around the edges of the cups, then unmold onto individual plates. Serve at once. ✳

INDEX